I0765090
This book belongs to....

Small preview of what's inside

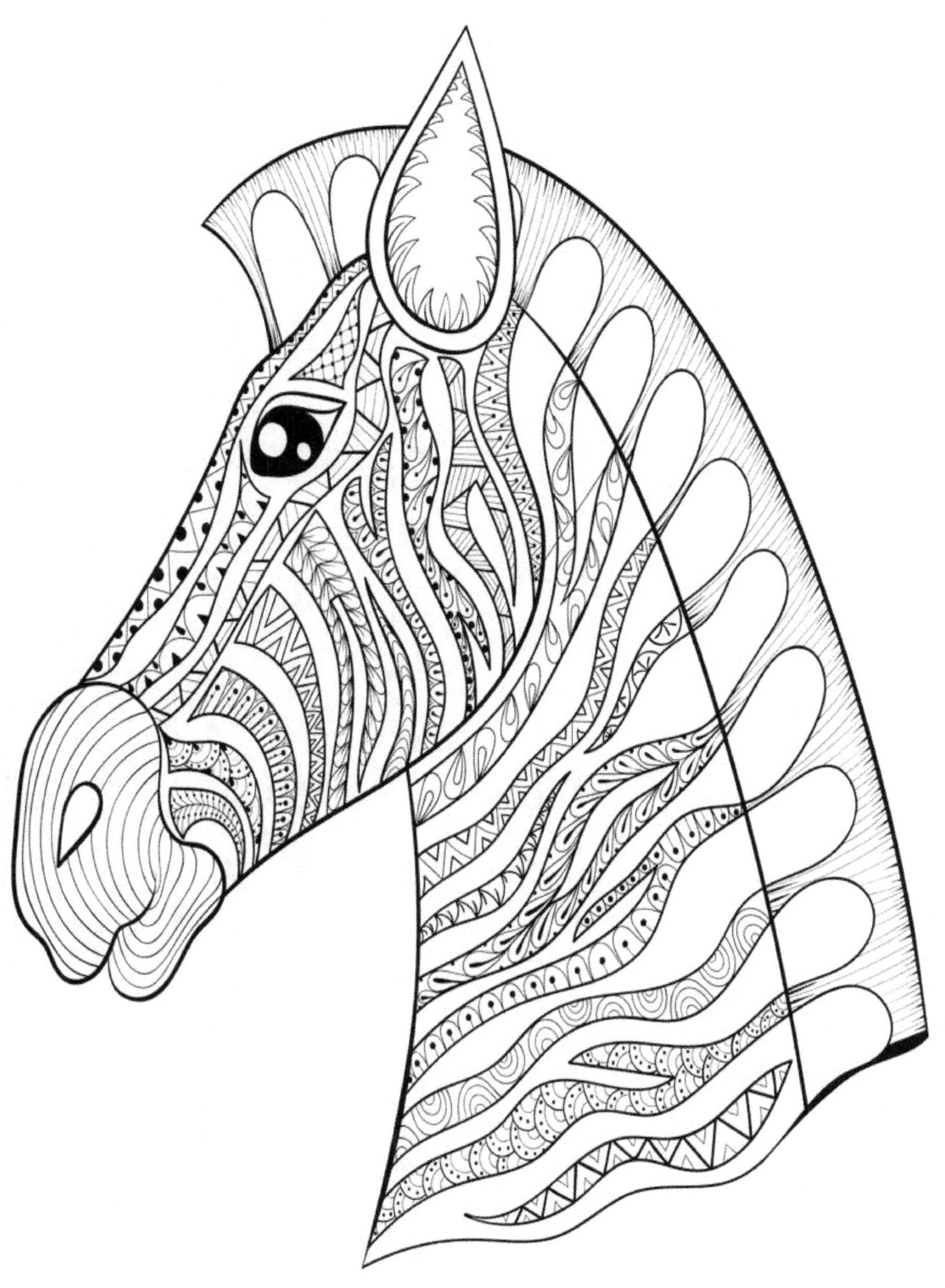

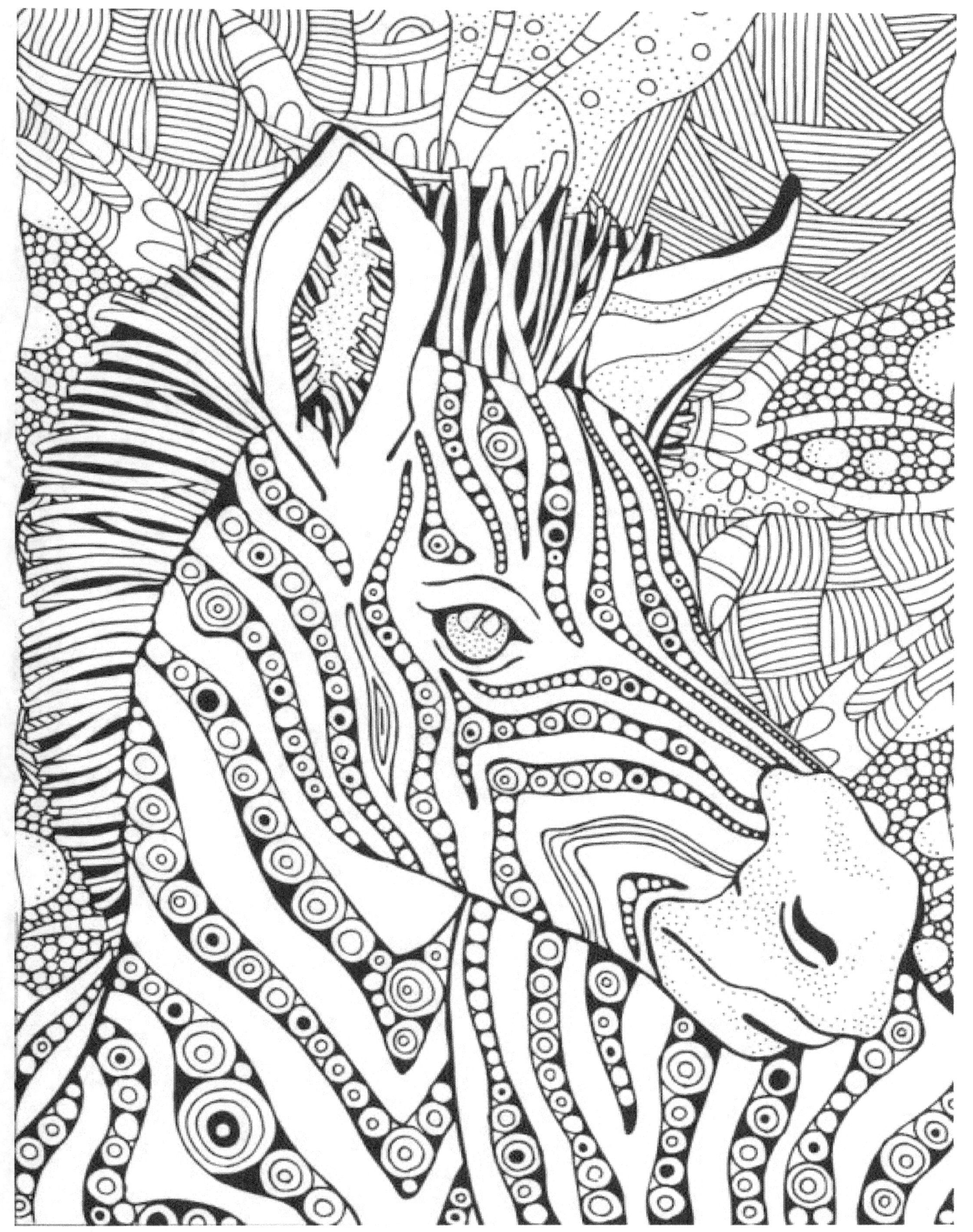

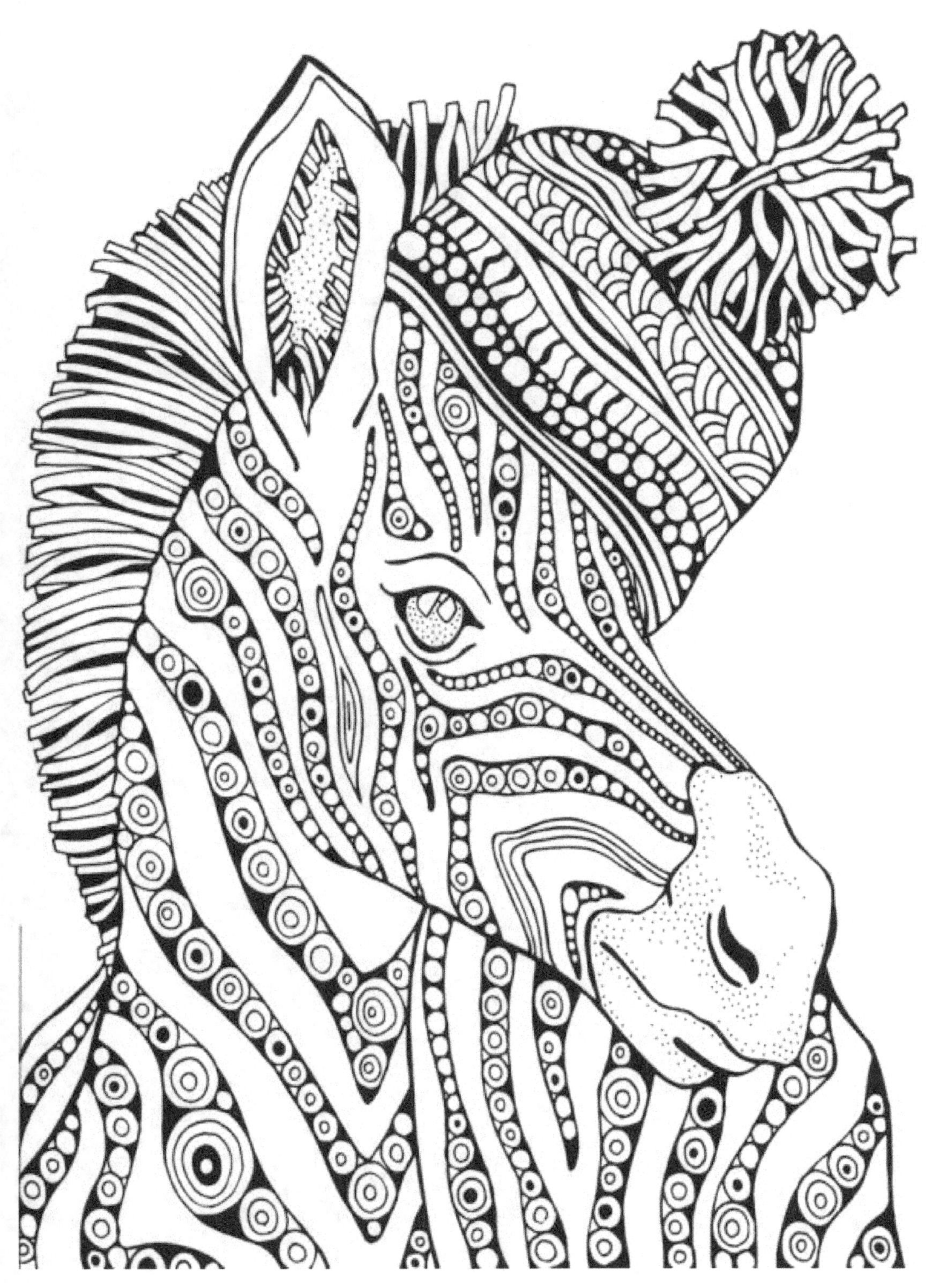

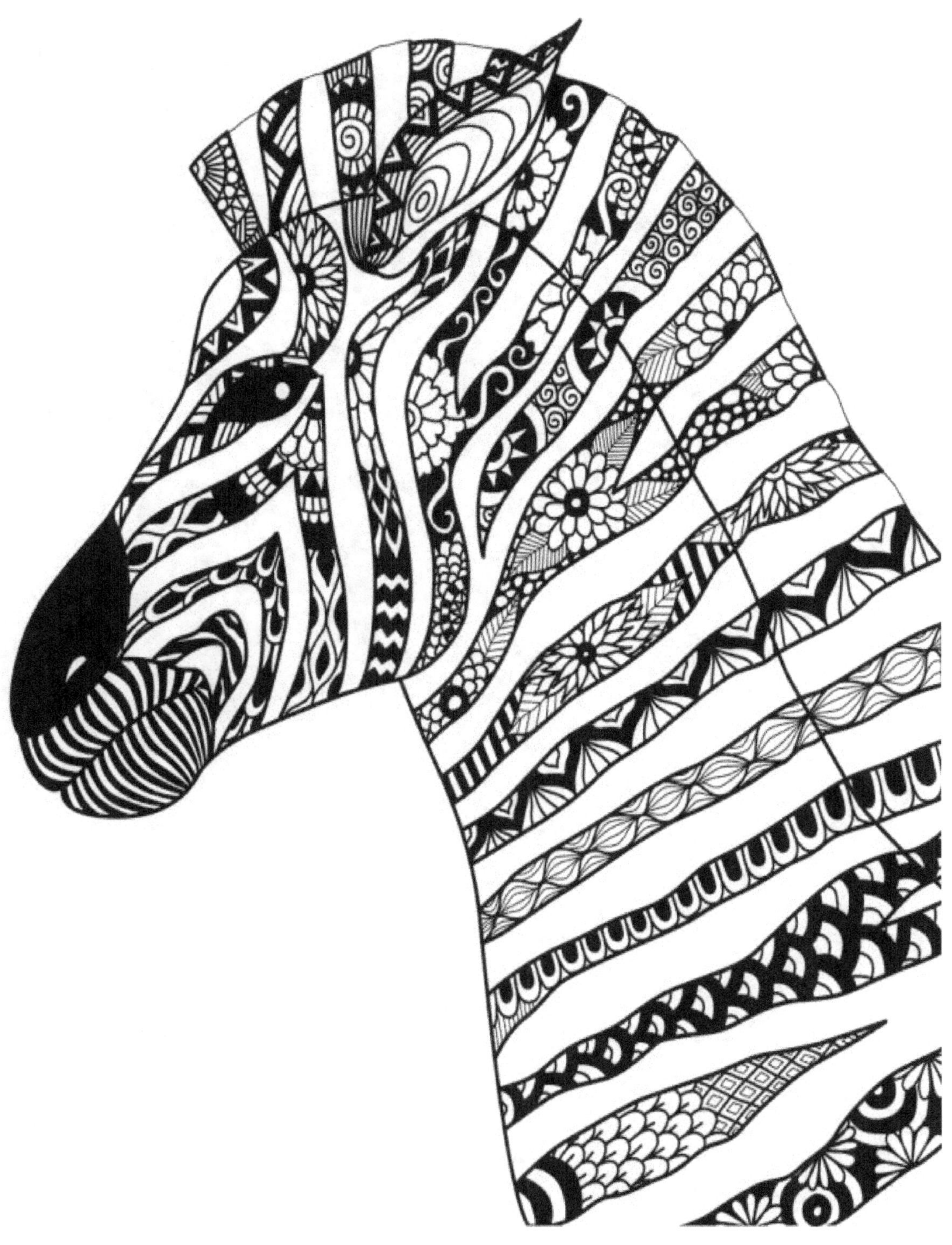

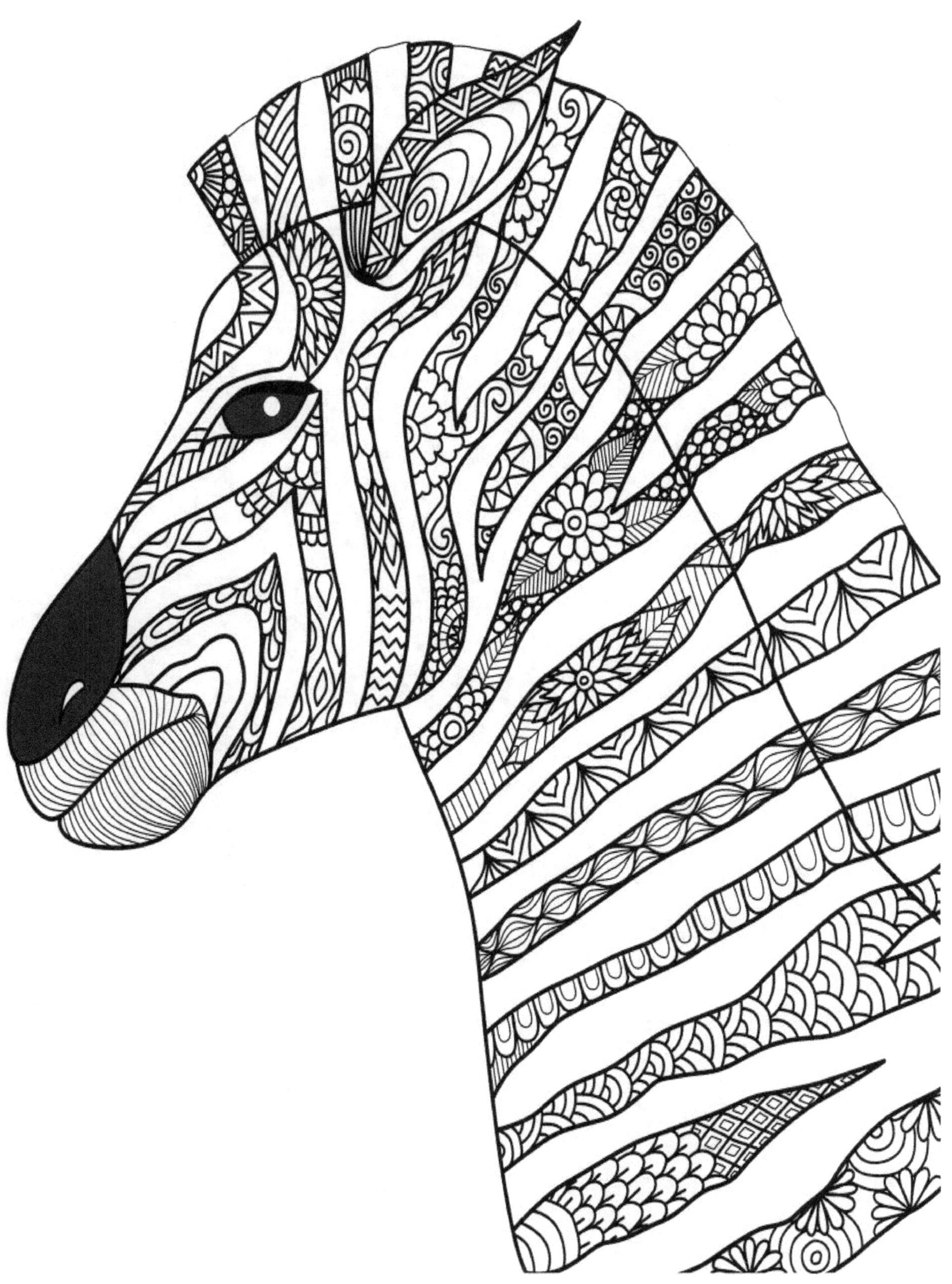

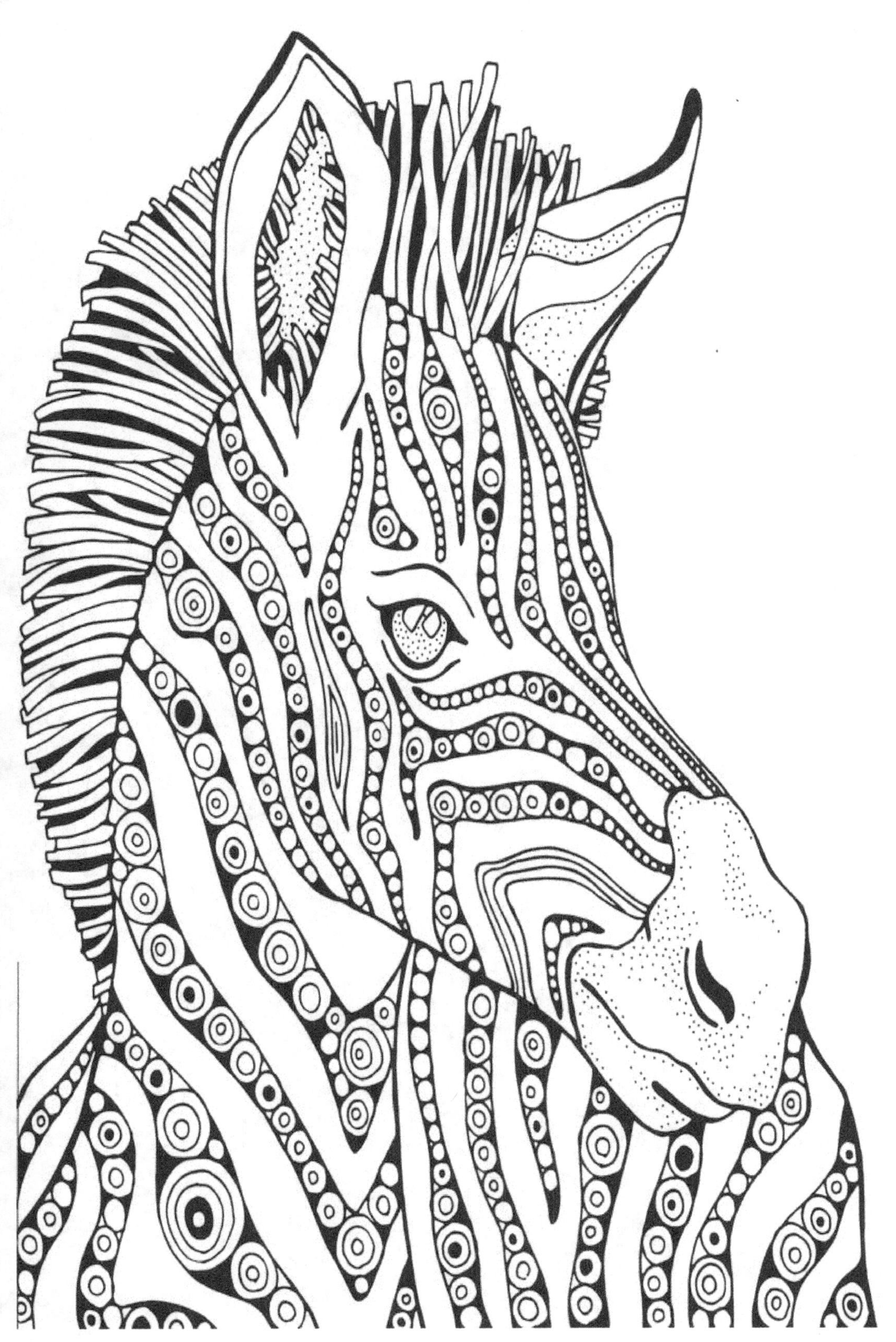

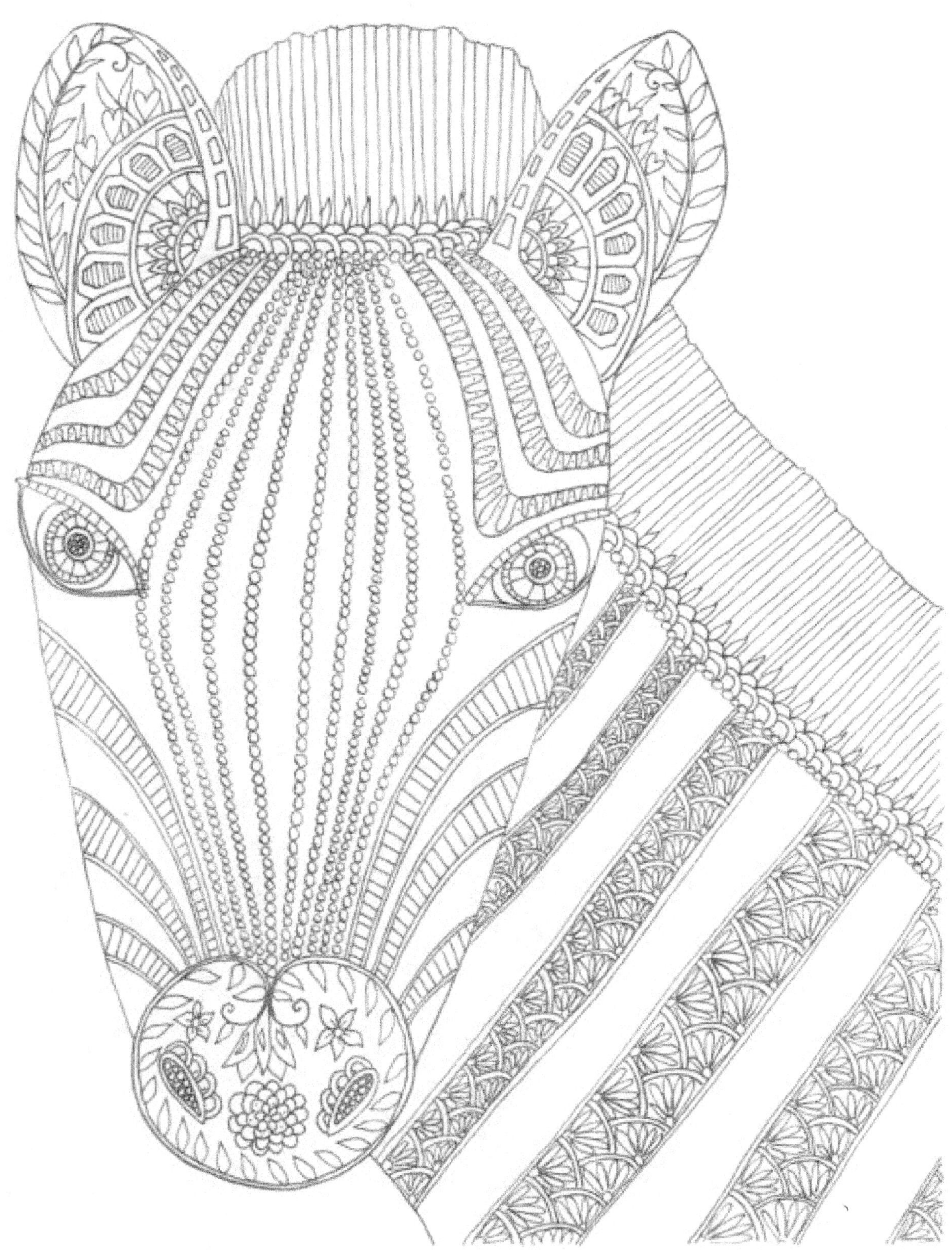

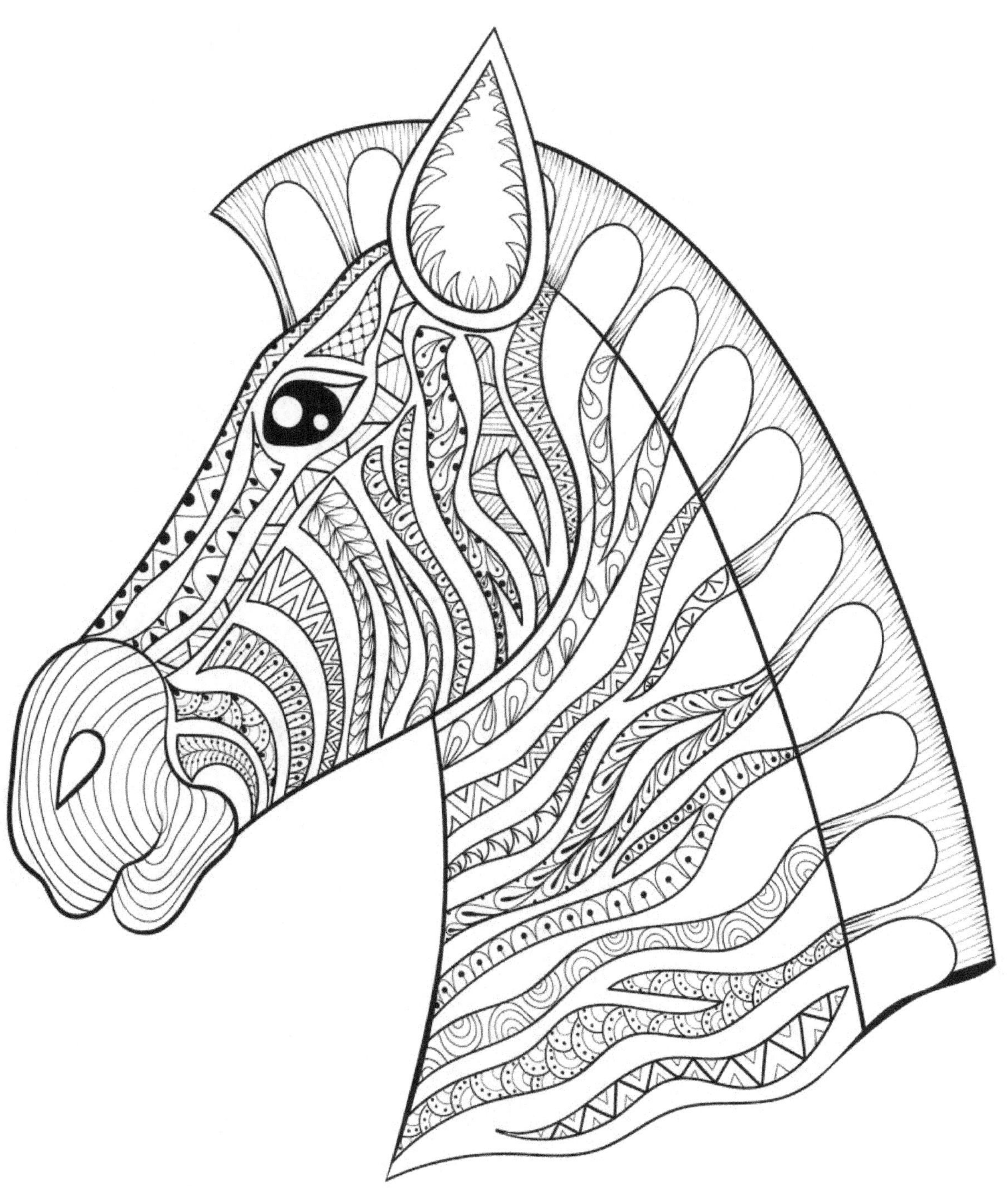

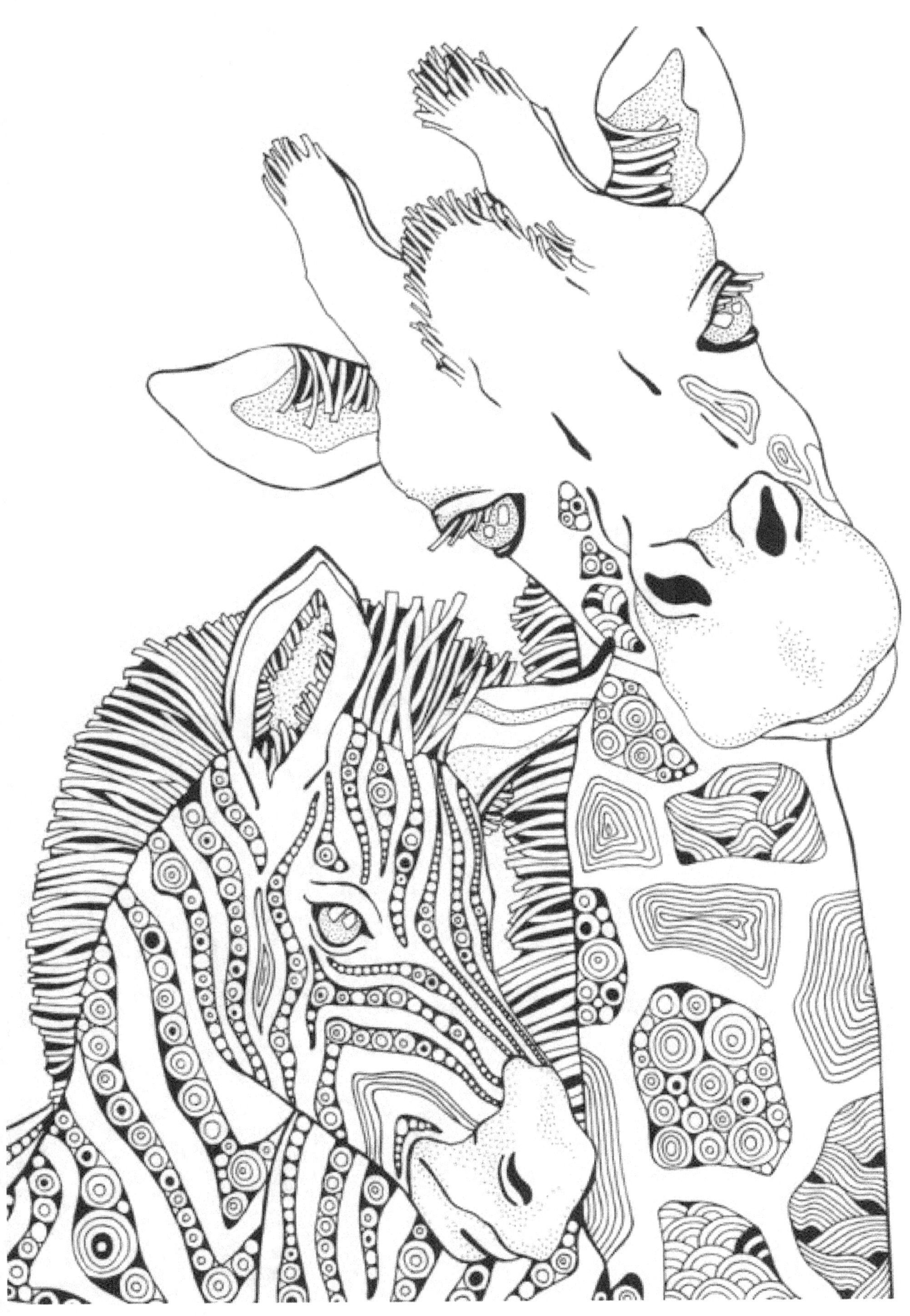

S